CHRISTMAS AT HOME

*Holiday
Card and
Letter Ideas*

Rebecca Germany

BARBOUR BOOKS
An Imprint of Barbour Publishing, Inc.

© 2002 by Barbour Publishing, Inc.

ISBN 1-58660-545-3

Cover image © Brand X Pictures

Published by Barbour Books, an imprint of Barbour Publishing, Inc., P.O. Box 719, Uhrichsville, Ohio 44683, www.barbourbooks.com

Member of the
Evangelical Christian
Publishers Association

Printed in Canada.

Special thanks to Cathy Marie Hake,
brainstormer extraordinaire,
and her daughter Kelly
who added many ideas to the mix.

Why do we go above and beyond to send those annual Christmas sentiments?

*"Feeling gratitude and not expressing
it is like wrapping a present and not giving it."*

WILLIAM ARTHUR WARD

Christmas is the universal time when we make that special effort to connect with family and friends whom we don't see on a regular basis. It falls at the end of the calendar year, and we naturally want to catch others up on what has been happening in our lives. Christmas is also one of the few times when non-Christian friends will allow Christians the freedom to remind them of Christ's real presence in the world.

The tradition of sending commercialized Christmas cards began in the Victorian era in London. Sir Henry Cole, director of the Victoria and Albert Museum, found he didn't have time to send a personal letter to all his friends and family at Christmastime. In December 1843, he asked painter John Callcott Horsley to design a card for him. One thousand cards were printed in lithography and hand colored. Cole sold his extra cards for a shilling apiece.

By the 1880s, the postal services in England and the United States were seeing a trend developing and advertised with "Post Early for Christmas" signs. Painters like Louis Prang and series like Currier & Ives increased the popularity of Christmas cards, and high-quality cards became mass produced.

Early cards were not only beautiful but elaborate in shape and design. They came as fans, stars, or scrolls. Some had silk and glitter finishes. Still others were "animated" by the pull of a tab.

These types of cards quickly replaced the handwritten notes that had been traditionally exchanged. Now almost everyone from families and individuals to businesses and nonprofit organizations sends out Christmas greetings by card or letter.

So dust off your address books and get back in touch with folks far and near.

"Greet all the saints in Christ Jesus."

PHILIPPIANS 4:21

Contents

Getting Organized

"Remember this:
Whoever sows sparingly will also reap sparingly,
and whoever sows generously will also reap generously."

2 CORINTHIANS 9:6

The Address Book

It is best to keep your address list updated throughout the year as you are made aware of changes, but if your list is out of shape, sit down before the Thanksgiving rush and get everything organized.

Electronic Address Book

If you want a future time saver, invest time now to enter all those addresses on your contact list into the computer. Once you have them stored you can do amazing things with the information. You'll have addresses handy for letters and envelopes. You can print out sheets of address labels and save handwriting. You can sort and share addresses easily. Updates are quick, without the mess of whiteout, erasers, and pen scratches.

Points of Preparation

- Before Thanksgiving is even over, consider your plans for sending Christmas greetings.
- Check that your address list is up-to-date and prepare your mailing list.
- Decide on the type of greeting—store-bought card, homemade card, postcard, newsy letter, E-mail, etc.
- Will you include a family photo? Portrait or snapshot?

- Will you prepare a special message—one-line statement of faith, paragraph of cheer, or letter-length update?
- Will you be tucking anything extra in with your greeting?
- Determine the time needed for preparing the mailing.
- How much will the mailing cost?
- Determine overall cost for what you want to do before buying.
- Set date for having your greetings in the mail.
- Make a plan for getting the greeting of choice bought or made and the personalizing, addressing, sealing, and mailing done.

Rank Your List

Go through your list of friends, relatives, acquaintances, business associates, neighbors, service providers, etc. Include everyone from old high school friends to your baby-sitter. Beside each name place a ranking of A, B, or C (A—must send, B—want to keep contact, C—not necessary).

Contact Cards

You've got your address book for handy reference, but to expedite handling of the Christmas greeting process, you need a system. Get a little box and a package of index cards. On one side write the person's name, family names, address, E-mail address, and other relevant information. On the other side, make a chart. Across the top, make 5–10 columns where the years will be placed. Along the left side make two catagories—sent and received. Each year mark when you send a greeting and if you have received a greeting. File by A-B-C ranking as mentioned before, then in alphabetical order.

What Type of Greeting Suits You?

Deciding what sort of greeting you will send this year could be the hardest or most enjoyable part of the process. Store-bought card, homemade card, postcard, newsy letter, E-mail, etc. Commercial cards will be in the stores by Thanksgiving, if you don't already have a stash of cards bought on clearance last January. Plan to buy early while selections are good. There are always those mail-order companies that will print your name on their cards. Postcards, bought or made, make quick

and efficient greetings. Then there is the pride of hand-crafting a greeting card with your personal touch. You can always recapture the year in a letter chock-full of news. Lastly there is the electronic time-saving means of the Internet. And you may have even considered other methods of sending greetings. Pick a method of sending holiday cheer that bests fits your allotted time and capabilities. Consider your budget. Also, try to have your greeting be a nice representation of who you are.

Family Photo

Plan ahead for a portrait shoot with a photographer. Allow time for setting up the appointment and getting the photos back. A snapshot would do nicely, though, for a Christmas greeting. Digital cameras make the process quick and easy with results immediately ready for viewing.

Photo Theme

Consider doing a theme in the picture. Coordinate what everyone is wearing with the background. Try having everyone in front of the Christmas tree wearing antlers. Use a rural landscape in the background and have everyone in denim. Be creative and represent your family interests and personalities in the photo.

Meaningful Message

Rarely can you find the perfect store-bought card that says all you want to say in your Christmas greeting. Most people want to add a personal note—even if they like the card's sentiment. Decide if you have a certain message to give to everyone this year. It could be one line like "We wish you the joy of knowing Jesus throughout the year." You may want to have a basic paragraph of cheer that you'll put in each greeting, with flexibility to adapt to the recipient. Or, you can write a newsy letter. A letter can be your complete greeting, or it can be placed inside a card.

Creative Writing

Share your creative writing skills with your family and friends. Write a poem or short story full of holiday cheer. Write out a memory of Christmas past. Use your children's writing from school projects. Or find a story available without copyright infringement, like the history of the candy cane or a quote from Charles Dickens's *A Christmas Carol,* and use it as your greeting.

Holiday Web Page

For the computer savvy (or those with children who are), create a holiday web page and include the link to it in a personalized E-mail message. Use photos from throughout the year. Get free animated clip art and music downloads from various Internet sites.

Greeting Stuffers

It is always fun to add a little something in your greeting that will extend the cheer, last beyond the holidays, or become a keepsake. You may want to include:

- A teabag or envelope of cocoa with instructions for the recipient to enjoy a holiday time-out on you.
- A packet of seeds with instructions to start planting indoors and enjoy a touch of early spring.
- A Christmas ornament like a crocheted snowflake or other durable ornament you have made that will survive the mailing process.

Time Savers

- Have a printing company put your personalized greeting and signature on your store-bought cards. This requires planning ahead but makes the mailing process go more quickly.
- Type your address list into the computer and print clear address labels in a nice font instead of hand-writing all those addresses.
- Take cards along on jaunts to the doctor, on the train or bus commute, at a child's practice session, or anyplace where you would have a few minutes to personalize them.
- Type a family newsletter and photocopy onto colored paper.

Money Savers

- Use postcards—cheaper to mail and less space to have to fill in with greetings.
- Keep the contents of your envelope light-weight enough that one standard stamp will cover the postage.
- Make multiple copies of letters, pictures, and inserts with a photocopier rather than use your expensive computer ribbons.
- No need to place the family newsletter in an envelope. Just keep the contents to one page, then fold, tape the edge, and address.
- E-mail a letter or use free electronic cards for all those with Internet access.
- Narrow your list of names to only those relatives you can't be with. Skip the family and friends you will see in person. A hug is much better than a card anyway. For those you exchange gifts with, you can attach your message of greeting on the gift box.

Postage

- Checking postage on odd-shaped or full envelopes before mailing could save the hassle of returns. Also, you certainly don't want your greeting to arrive "postage due"!
- Buy holiday stamps.
- Don't put any loose materials like "angel dust" or "crystal snowflakes" in your envelope that may cause worry or mess to postal workers.

Make It a Working Party

See the "Creating Traditions" section. Plan a party to get the work of making cards, personalizing your greeting, labeling, sealing, stamping, and posting your Christmas cards and letters done through a fun and enjoyable process.

Thank-You Notes

Plan the thank-you notes before Christmas. In today's busy society, proper manners are often overlooked. A quick word of thanks and a hug after we open a Christmas gift is about all the giver gets. Determine to write a personal thank-you note to all who give you gifts this year. Help your children do the same. People love to be thanked and want to know their efforts were appreciated.

Homemade Cards and Stationery

*"I, Paul, write this greeting in my own hand,
which is the distinguishing mark in all my letters.
This is how I write."*

2 THESSALONIANS 3:17

Be like the apostle Paul and put a personal touch on your greetings.

Crafting Tips

Before starting your card, decide on the size and be sure you have an envelope to fit it. Office supply stores, mail-order stationery companies, and unique discount stores often carry packages of odd-sized envelopes.

Choose paper with beauty and durability. You want your card to be sturdy enough to stand up on a table.

Consider the mailing weight of the finished project.

Have a collection of templates like cookie cutters, glue, double-sided tape, plain and fancy scissors, paper punchers, stickers, glitter, and other embellishments on hand.

Creative Touches

Stamping
Sponge paint
Calligraphy
Paper punch designs
Stickers

Glitter
Spray snow
Computer clip art
Fancy-edged scissors
Wax seals

Unique Forms of Stationery

- Paper napkins, towels, bathroom tissue, tablecloth, plates, etc.
- T-shirt—Decorate a shirt with a greeting the receiver can wear.
- Post-It Notes—Write a separate message on each note. Have the recipient post the notes around home, the car, and the office as reminders of your holiday wishes for them.
- Wide ribbon
- Fabric
- Balloon
- Paper bag—for a message you can fill or an envelope you can stuff.

Marbleized Stationery

YOU WILL NEED:

Acrylic paint
Water
Paper cups
Liquid Starch
9"x13" baking pan
Paper towels

Construction paper or
  cardstock, preferably
  white
$1/8$" wide ribbon
Comb

In a paper cup, mix 2 tablespoons of paint with 2 tablespoons of water. Add more paint or water if necessary to make a creamy mixture. Pour enough starch into the baking pan, 1–1½ inches deep. Pat the surface with a paper towel to remove any air bubbles. Scatter several drops of paint mixture onto the starch. If paint sinks to the bottom of the pan, add more water to the paint. Use a comb to swirl the paint and starch mixture and make designs. Lay a sheet of paper on top of the mixture, letting the middle of the page touch first. Smooth the outside edges of the paper over the mixture. Allow it to sit approximately 15 seconds, then lift the paper from the paint. Lay it face up

on paper towels and lay a paper towel on top. Use the heel of your hand to press down on the paper towel, removing extra paint. Gently take the paper towel off and repeat the process with another paper towel. Allow the marbled paper to dry completely. Then trace and cut desired cookie cutter shapes from the paper. Rub a glue stick on the unpainted side and stick the backs of equal shapes together if desired (this would make a good ornament). For a card, you can fold the marbled paper in half, place your template against the fold, and cut out a shaped card. Or, you can glue marbled shapes to a plain card and embellish with ribbon, calligraphy, and glitter.

Wrapping-Paper Scraps

Use scraps of holiday wrapping paper to cover plain cards. Cut pieces to add color behind a photo or for framing photos that you attach to your cards.

Marble Chase Paper

Put white paper in a box with a flat bottom that is just a tad larger than the paper. Drop in a few marbles that have been dipped in red, green, and gold paint. Pick the box up and move it so the marbles roll around and create a fun design.

Multifolds

Think outside the normal single-fold card. Fold a sheet of paper twice, creating 3 equal sections like a brochure. Or fold each side in to meet in the middle and open like a double door.

Linked Cards

Fold your paper 2-3 times in accordion style. Cut a simple shape (tree, star, heart, ornament, etc) overlapping the folds on both sides. When unfolded several shapes should be connected in a chain.

Fabric-Designed Cards

8½" x11" card-weight paper
Fabric scraps
Fusible web material

An iron and ironing board
Calligraphy pen, markers, or
    fabric paint

Fold your paper in half to make a card (make sure you have an envelope to fit the size). Choose a simple design or shape to cut from the fabric. Cookie cutters make good patterns. Make a template for the fabric design out of heavy paper or light cardboard. Heat your iron.

Place fusible web with paper backing side down on the ironing board. Then place fabric, right side up, on top of fusible web. Cover fabric with a thin towel or ironing cloth. Iron the fabric and fusible web together, using an up and down motion, do not slide the iron. Press each area only a few seconds. Trace template pattern onto right side of fused fabric with pencil. Cut the design out just inside the lines. Fuse the fabric to card by peeling off the paper backing and placing the fabric shape on the card where you want it. Put a cloth on top and iron in the same pressing and lifting motion that you used before. (You can use more than one fabric shape per card, and you can overlap the designs.) Use markers, calligraphy pens, or fabric paint to embellish your card.

Work of Art

Get the artist, preferably a child, to draw a Christmas scene. Keep it colorful and use a colored photocopier or scanner to make copies for the front of your card.

Specially-Picked Pics

Using cards that you received last year, select pictures that match the receiver. Cut out the picture from the old card and mount it on a folded piece of colored paper to make a new card. Start your message with "I chose this picture for you because. . ." Snow could be a reminder of times you played with the recipient as a child. Jesus in the manger could be a reminder that this person impacted your relationship with Christ. This card idea is a special way to make your greeting personal and meaningful.

Embossed Cards

Find a simple shape like those of cookie cutters. Trace it onto a piece of thin cardboard. Create a stencil by cutting out the center (using a utility knife works best). Cut a piece of construction paper to size for a card and fold in half. Unfold and pick the spot to emboss. Lay the paper on the stencil, hold in place, and use the rounded end of a craft stick to gently rub the paper into the shape. Remove from stencil and finish the card with your message.

Window Cards

Fold a rectangle of cardstock in half. On the front side trace a simple shape using a light touch with a pencil. Unfold the card and lay it on a cutting surface. Use a utility knife to cut the design out. Leave the shaped window open to show your message on the inside or cover it from the backside with fabric, colored cellophane, lace, photo, child's artwork, or other paper. Use a paper punch to add little windows around the large one (i.e. little stars around a tree). Use a different covering behind those windows. On the backside of your windows where your window patches are glued on, you may want to cover this area with a plain piece of paper to hide the magic of the front window design.

Sewn Cards

Remember the sewing cards from preschool days? Refresh those skills. Cut a shape from heavy paper. Punch holes approximately ¼ inch from the edge and ½ inch apart. Go all around the shape. Thread ribbon or cording through the holes and tie at the top. Glue the shape to a plain card. Or, you can do the sewing directly to the front of your card. Plain cards work well with your own message hand-written in the center, but some store-bought designs could also be embellished with ribbon.

Puzzle Card

Mount a photo or piece of artwork on sturdy paper or use an old Christmas card front. Write your holiday message on the back, then cut the card into 6–12 pieces. Place them in an envelope and mail. (You might want to place small puzzle pieces in a plastic bag before tucking it into the envelope.) Recipients will enjoy assembling your greeting.

Snowflake Card

Have fun alone or with the kids experimenting with cutting small snowflakes from white paper. Use a brush to smooth a thin layer of glue over the back and glue to a dark blue cardstock.

December Wishes

Save those calendars that every organization and business gives out at the beginning of the year or buy calendars that go on clearance at the end of the year. Take out the "December" page. Write "I wish for you. . ." at the top of the page and a Christmas wish on each day (i.e. "good shopping" or "time to read Luke 1–2").

Family Hands Card

Trace Dad's hand onto your card front and have Mom trace her hand inside Dad's. Then trace the kids, starting with the largest hand inside Mom's hand. Use a different color to outline each hand. Or create templates of each hand and cut each one out of a different color of paper. Starting with Dad's, or the largest, glue the hands one on top of the other, adding the smallest last.

Hand Wreath Card

Have your kids make 5–6 handprints from green construction paper. Glue them overlapping on a 2 inch-wide, rigid paper ring. Glue on a red ribbon bow that will flatten for mailing. Sign the back with a Christmas greeting. Give to relatives (especially grandparents) and they can use the card as a decoration.

Candle Cards

Buy a pack of birthday candles and colored construction paper or card-stock. Cut an 8"x10" paper in half. Fold each half in half again to form a card. Using transparent tape, secure a candle to the front of the card. Write a message like "Jesus is the light of the world" or "May the light of Christmas warm your holidays."

Holiday Rubs

Place a sheet of typing or other lightweight paper over an old embossed Christmas card. Using a crayon or two, rub the design until it appears on your paper. Trim the design area you want to use. Mount it onto colored construction paper that is slightly larger than your design. Paste the colored picture on a folded card and print your Christmas message inside.

Nature Impressions

Gather some leaves and flowers (lacy fronds of ferns work well). Place a sheet of white or cream colored cardstock on a newspaper-coated surface. Lay your bits of nature on the sheet. Spray a light coat of paint over the whole sheet of paper (light green is nice). Let the paint partially dry before removing the leaves and flowers. Their impressions should be evident in the unpainted areas of the paper. Use the paper as stationery for your greeting cards.

4 Seasons

Take a picture of the same place during each of the four seasons. Or have the family artist draw the scenes. It could be a spot in your yard or a local landscape. Create a trifold card. Fold a large sheet of paper in half, unfold, then fold the edges to meet at the middle fold. Across the front that looks like a double door, write "God's love never changes." Find 1–4 Scripture verses to place on each inside panel with the pictures.

He's Got the Whole World in His Hands

When it's been a tough year for the family and country, focus on God's provision. Use a picture of His hands holding the world. Inside the flap of the card, list victories, challenges, hopes, dreams, and concerns of your family, and at the bottom, include a verse about trusting the Lord. You could also make a 3-D card and attach the globe over the hands on a flap that can be lifted. Under the globe, place a picture of your family.

The Gift of Gab

Glue string and a small, flattened paper cup on the front of a blank card and write, "I miss your voice at this time of year." Inside write "Those were the olden days. Today's solution. . ." and tape a prepaid calling card below the words. Send to a faraway friend, relative, or college student.

Activity Cards

Create a card that will bring enjoyment to the children on your contact list. Design the front of your card to entertain the youngsters.
Use a drawing for the front design that kids can color. Or create a
dot-to-dot design. Outline a relatively simple shape with a series of
dots. Number the dots in the order that the connecting lines should
be drawn. Kids draw the line to reveal the picture you have sent with
your greeting.

Doll Greeting

Design a card that is the shape of a paper doll. Take it to an office supply place and have several copies printed on heavy paper. Include costumes for her to be dressed as an angel or as Mary holding baby Jesus.

Coupon Cards

Create a card design with 1–2 homemade coupons that can be torn off and redeemed by family, neighbors, and local friends. Promise to make yourself available for:

raking leaves	taking out the trash
shoveling snow	baby-sitting
walking the dog	dinner out at a favorite
washing the car	restaurant

From Our House to Yours

An especially nice way to show off your new or remodeled home. Have the artist in your family draw a picture of your house and a picture of the nativity. Or take a photo of your house and use a nice picture of the nativity that you have permission to copy. On the front of your card, write "From the manger to the world" and glue the nativity picture below. On the inside flap of the card, write "From our house to yours" and glue the picture of your house below. On the back, inside flap, write "His love is to be shared by all."

Christmas "Fortune" Cards

Put a recipe for fortune cookies on the front of your card. For the message of your card, say something like "A taste of heaven was our fortune on that first Christmas."

Include a list of "fortune" lines, perhaps on a separate sheet enclosed in your card.

- "Wise men still seek Him."
- "God loves you. So do I."
- "Love cometh from heaven. . .and also from the person across the room."
- "Today is the birth date of Joy."

Fortune Cookies

5 tbsp unsalted butter
4 egg whites
1 c super fine sugar
1 c sifted all-purpose flour

1 pinch salt
3 tbsp heavy
    whipping cream
1 tsp almond extract

Preheat oven to 400°. Spray a cookie sheet with oil. In a small saucepan, melt butter over low heat. In a large bowl, combine egg whites and sugar; then beat on medium speed for about 30 seconds. Blend in the flour and salt. Add melted butter, cream, and extract; beat until mixed. Pour 1 tablespoon of batter onto one side of the baking pan. Use a spoon to spread it into a thin 5-inch circle. Make another circle on other half of the pan. Bake approximately 8 minutes or until the edges turn golden brown. Place baking pan on a heat-resistant surface. Working quickly, slide a spatula under one cookie. Lift and place on a dishtowel. Fold cookie in half, pinching at top to form loose semicircle. Insert index fingers into ends; press indentation into center of cookie while bending ends together to form shape of a fortune cookie. (To help keep the shape in place, sit the folded cookie in a muffin tin cup while it cools.) Once the cookie hardens, you cannot fold it. Repeat with the rest of the batter until you have approximately 15 cookies. Write your message on long strips of sturdy paper and thread it through the cooled cookie.

Toothless Grin

Take a close-up picture of your 5 to 6 year old's toothless smile. Glue it on the front of your card and write an "All I want for Christmas. . ." caption under it. Inside, list the blessings you most want for yourself, your family and friends, and the world in general.

Free Printable Cards

On the Internet there are several sites that have free printable cards and gift tags. You can personalize them and print them out. Some come in color, and some are just black lines that you can color in or leave as they are.

Homemade Envelopes

waxed freezer paper   ironing board
tissue paper   glue stick
iron   one envelope

Find an envelope the size and shape of the ones you want to make. Carefully take it apart at the seams, smooth it flat, and trace it onto poster board. Cut this out for your template. Crumple up a sheet of tissue paper, then smooth it flat over the waxed side of a sheet of freezer paper. Put your iron on low with no steam, and iron with light pressure until the two surfaces bond. Trace the envelope template

onto back of the freezer paper and cut out. Fold the new envelope and use stick glue to seal the seams.

OR

Remake a heavy sheet of wrapping paper or a wall calendar picture into an envelope. Make an envelope template in a size that will best display the design or picture on your paper, place it on your paper where you will make best use of the paper's art on the envelope front, and trace it. Cut it out, fold the new envelope, and use stick glue to seal the seams. Use mailing labels so your addresses will be clearly seen over the design.

*The true spirit of Christmas is not about spending—
it's about giving—
from the heart more than from the pocketbook."*

ANONYMOUS

Keepsake Greetings

"For where your treasure is, there your heart will be also."

Luke 12:34

Ornament Cards

Paper Design—Use a simple shape and cut it out of red or green poster board. Decorate both sides with glued-on glitter, sequins, lace, and the like. Punch a hole in the top and tie on a gold thread hanger. Attach the ornament to the front or inside flap of your homemade or store-bought greeting card by placing tape across the thread.

Cross-stitch Art—Make a small and simple holiday design by cross-stitch. Create a frame for it with light cardboard. Make a hole for a hanger. Attach the back of the ornament to the front of a homemade card using double-sided tape.

Sparkling Glue—Trace cookie cutter shapes onto plain paper. Place waxed paper over the design and outline it with glue. Coat the surface of the shape with glue and fill it with glitter (suggest ultra-fine variety). Let dry for several days. Cut the shape out and repeat glue and glitter on the reverse side. When completely dry, make a hole in the top and create a hanger with thread or thin ribbon. Attach the ornament to the front or inside flap of your homemade or store-bought greeting card by placing tape across the hanger.

Golden Stars—Buy a piece of metal window screen, gold spray paint, gold fabric paint, and gold thread. Spray the screen and let it dry. With a sharp permanent marker, draw or trace a star shape onto the screen. Cut out using old scissors. Squeeze fabric paint from the bottle onto the rough edge, creating a solid, raised line. Lay on waxed paper to dry. When dry, check that both sides of the edge have a solid line of paint. Apply more if needed. To the center, apply a design or write a word like "joy" or someone's name. Attach a thread hanger. Fasten the ornament to the front or inside flap of your homemade or store-bought greeting card by placing tape across the thread.

Crocheted Snowflakes—Use your crocheting skills to make snowflakes or small doilies. (Short cut and buy some small doilies if you must.) Starch them. Attach a coordinating floss hanger. Fasten the ornament to the front or inside flap of your homemade or store-bought greeting card by placing tape across the floss.

Tin Punches—Save the lids from concentrated juice cans. Wash well. Use a hammer and nail to "tin punch" a design into them—a cross, heart, or star work especially well. Hot glue lace and ribbon around it. Glue a paper on the back—or use a self-adhesive label—with your greeting and the date on it.

Bookmark Greeting

Buy or make bookmarks that you can send in place of a card. As the recipients use the bookmark during the year, they'll think of you. Homemade bookmarks can be fancy like cross-stitched work or as simple as construction paper reinforced with clear contact paper. Be sure to date and sign the back.

Magnets

Custom-make a message that will be a yearlong reminder of your love. Buy adhesive-backed magnets at an office supply store. Write your greeting on a cardboard shape and affix the magnet to the back.

First Christmas Card

Send cards from your family's newborn. Get his/her footprint, scan it into the computer and color it red or green. Add a message that says something like this: *Christmas is about a Baby. . .first, in Bethlehem. . . and now, a tiny part of that gift arrived from heaven again. . .* Print it on cardstock.

A New Life

For the family on your mailing list who has a new baby, make a card that contains one of each coin minted that year or one of each postage stamp printed that year.

Recipe Card

Choose a recipe you are known for doing well or one that has been passed down through your family as an heirloom. Set it up nicely by writing on a recipe card or using your computer. Dress it up with holiday clip art and add color in the lettering and art. If using a recipe card, mount it with a bit of double-sided tape onto a folded card that is a little larger than the recipe card. If printing the recipe from the computer, print directly onto cardstock and design your greeting so that the recipe on the front of the card can be detached from your greeting.

Calendar Card

Create a 12-page booklet—homemade calendar—by folding 7 sheets of paper in half. Put your holiday greeting on page one. Use family photos to personalize the area in and around the calendar chart. Add family dates of birthdays, anniversaries, and special events. Keep the calendar small enough to fit an envelope for mailing.

Functional Greeting

Several design companies will print your family's picture on coffee mugs, computer mouse pads, jigsaw puzzles, coasters, apparel, calendars, and the like. These items are ideal Christmas greetings for far-away grandparents.

Or do your own designing. Give school-aged kids/teens fabric paints and let them design a greeting on handkerchiefs, aprons, bread warmers, potholders, or book bags as usable holiday gifts. They can also use a quilter's "purple pen" to write a greeting on the gift and include a note telling the recipient to dab the ink away with a damp sponge before using it.

Fun Photo Flip Card

Get a full-face picture of each family member (dog and cat, too). Scan the photos into the computer and adjust so that they all are the same size (try 4"x4"). Print onto cardstock and trim each picture equal size and with at least ½ inch on the left side of each picture. Compile them in a stack, including a blank piece of cardstock at the bottom. Then carefully glue the left edges together using no more than a ½-inch strip of glue. When dry, cut across each picture equally so you can flip sections and have Dad's eyes, Mom's nose, Junior's mouth, and other silly combinations. Don't cut the blank piece. Use it as the reinforcing base of your flip card and as space for writing your greeting.

Photo Album Card

Create a little booklet of family photos. Show highlights from the year and/or picture each family member on their own page with descriptions of their age, hobbies, and the like. Let each family member put a personal greeting by his or her photo. (Pictures that are computer-printed or photocopied onto standard paper will be lighter in weight for mailing than actual photo shop prints.)

Music Card

Use the words from an old Christmas hymn in the message of your card. Include a cassette or CD recording of your family singing a few carols.

Video Card

Produce a family video card. Almost all American homes have VCRs. Not everyone has a video recorder, but you probably know someone from whom you can borrow one. Record each member giving his or her holiday greeting. Have someone sing or play a song. Someone else could do a cheer or show a talent for drama. Edit the greetings together and include snippets from family activities—Dad washing the car, Junior playing baseball, Baby in the kiddy pool, the family trimming the tree.

The Holiday Newsletter

*"You yourselves are our letter, written on our hearts,
known and read by everybody."*

2 CORINTHIANS 3:2

It isn't necessary to send a traditional Christmas card if you send a Christmas letter. No need to fret over how to make the contents interesting, either. Just pick an idea from here.

He Is Great and I Am Small

Use Daddy's footprint next to the littlest child's. Stamp, trace, cut and paste, or copy the feet onto stationery paper. Use "He Is Great and I Am Small" as the theme of your family letter, describing how God has gotten the family through the year.

Story Theme

Pretend you are Hans Christian Anderson and write the fairytale of your family's life. "Once upon a time there was a little house on a narrow street in a tiny town. In that house lived a man who left each morning to report to a mean giant of a boss at a towering accounting building. But each evening he arrived home to the sweet smells of home-microwaved boxed meals and the sounds of children arguing. For in that house with him lived a petite snip of a woman who. . ."

Wanted Poster

Place your child's fall school picture under the heading of "wanted." List the particulars on the child like name, nickname, height, weight, etc. Give "place last seen" as in "third grade." Share the child's hobbies as "known to frequent soccer fields and choir rooms." Or picture the whole family as a notoriously wanted gang last seen in the family room playing Scrabble.

Olympics Theme

Play off a popular Olympic year and portray the areas your family members are "winners" in.

- Junior is getting Gold in Auto Racing—"new" used gold car to drive
- Sis is getting Silver in Smiles—new braces
- Baby is getting Bronze in Walking—bronzed the shoes she took her first steps in on _____

And include the "Photo Finish" with a family picture at the bottom of the letter!

Musical Theme

Have each family member pick a hymn or song to represent him or her and their year. Use the song to title their paragraph of the newsletter.

Garden Theme

What's growing at your house? Kids' growth notes. News on expanded pet, car, states visited, and similar collections. Maybe family members have been gaining patience and other fruits of the Spirit. Provide news about the growth process. Perhaps there has been a new baby "harvested" in the family. Use clip art in the letter to enhance the garden environment.

"Walk a Mile" Theme

Use the headline "Walk a Mile in Our Shoes" on your letter. Pick a shoe to represent each family member (in general—heels for mama, sneakers for kids, flip-flops for teens, booties for baby, or for hobbies—cowboy boots, hiking boots, ballerina slippers, tap shoes, fisher's hip boots, and so on). Use clip art of footwear, shoestrings, and the like. You could even stamp the treads of sneakers onto your stationery.

Light Theme

Place a clip art string of Christmas lights across the top of your letter. Select a different light symbol for each family member and use the clipart with each person's news article.

- Light bulb—Sis graduated with honors and got full scholarship to Oxford.
- Flashlight—Junior went on his first Boy Scout campout.
- Candle—Grandpa finally gave his heart to the Lord.
- Star—Dad got promoted at work.

For the Family on the Go

Headline your letter with a line like "We're Always on the Go." Find a vehicle picture to use for each member of the family (i.e. Mom's taxi, Dad's boat, Junior's go-cart, Sister's bike, and Baby's walker). Dip the wheels of a toy car in paint and embellish your stationery with wheel tracks.

Party Hat

Write or print your annual letter on the backside of a piece of heavy quality Christmas wrapping paper. Feature each family member as a type of hat—mortarboard for the graduate, party hat for a sweet 16, baseball cap for the little leaguer, bonnet for baby. Fold the letter up like a party hat and slip into a card-sized envelope.

Pet Fetish

For folks who have a special pet—use the pet's paw print for art and write the letter from the pet's point of view.

THEY went to Barbados.
    I went to the kennel.
THEY had a barbecue for Junior's graduation.
    I had kibble.
THEY saw Fourth of July fireworks at Disney World.
    I saw only the laundry room and listened to the dryer buzzer for eight hours.
THEY went on a work and witness team to Mexico.
    I barked at the neighbor's Chihuahua.

Puzzle

Create a crossword puzzle with hints for your family's events.

    1 across: Junior is in _ _ _ _ _ grade
    1 down: Sis plays this instrument.

Provide a list of keywords that are the answers.

Or, design a word search with a block of words dedicated to each family member.

Mom—gardener, reads, drives kid's taxi, great baker, piano. . .
Dad—policeman, little league coach, church usher, computer
    junkie. . .

Magazine

Make a multiple-page card. Create a feature story about one special event or an article that summarizes the year. Use spotlight articles on each family member. Include a letter from the "editor." Since every magazine has advertisements, include an ad for coming events (i.e. Sis is getting married in June, or Junior opens baseball season as catcher).

He Said, She Said

A couple could do a trifold letter with a "He Said" column on one flap, a "She Said" on the other, and the "Truth" in the middle.

He Said—I'm a great carpenter.
She Said—He's a maintenance disaster.
Truth—His dad helped with adding on the new deck. He cut his leg with the saw and spent most of the time watching his dad from a lawn chair.

Empty Nesters

Use a bird theme in the artwork of your letter. Include a small article on each bird that has flown (college kids and young married couples often don't take time to communicate their life's happenings). Include a headline message like "That First Christmas, God gave His Son so we could be free from sin. . . This Christmas, we realize, with our nest empty, the magnitude of His sacrifice." Fold a tiny feather in with your letter that will float out when the letter is opened and read.

Police Report

View your family life from the eyes of investigating officers. Have fun considering how silly some of your family activities and habits might look to outsiders.

Investigating address 115 W. Fourth Street:
  Teen son's room: Looks ransacked. Clearly has affinity for blue
      jeans and electronic gadgets.
  Baby daughter's room: Pink explosion. Obviously a pampered
      princess.
  Kitchen: Faint smell of recent fire. Remains of murdered dinner in
      sink. Neighbors say the family is at McDonald's again.

Caricatures

Have an artist do a silly character-type sketch of each member of the family. Scan and reduce them with your computer. Use them for the photos along with silly descriptions of family life in your newsletter.

Circus

Write a headline like "Our life is a circus. We're always juggling. . ." Then do snippets for each family member including words like juggle, three-ring, high wire, clowns, and so on.

Frugal Letter Tips

- Keep your Christmas letter under one page in length to save on paper and photocopying costs. (How much do people really want to know about you, anyway? A short paragraph about each family member should be sufficient.)
- Make a collage of pictures to photocopy on the backside of the letter.
- Make multiple copies of letters, pictures, and inserts with a photocopier rather than your expensive computer ribbons.
- No need to place the family newsletter in an envelope. Just keep the contents to a one-sided page, then fold, tape the edge, and address.

Christmas ties us to the past.
We celebrate the good years and the bad,
the long bleak eras that slowly but surely brought us to today."

ALEXANDER PHILLIPS

Greeting Sentiments

*"I hope to see you soon, and we will talk face to face.
Peace to you. The friends here send their greetings.
Greet the friends there by name."*

3 JOHN 1:14

The following are ideas for text you can use inside your homemade
cards.

Food for Thought

May the wish of your heart be granted this Christmas season.

May the deep, abiding love that allows miracles to happen
live in your heart.

Take Christ with you.
Don't leave Him in the manger.

Born a child.
Died a man.
Rose a Savior.

He came that we might have abundant life.

I pray for you to know. . .

- Blessed wonder like Mary knew when the angel Gabriel visited her.
- Reverent awe that Joseph had upon waking from his dream.
- Delight as Elizabeth felt when her child leaped in recognition of Mary and her expected son.
- Amazement comparable to what brought the shepherds to their knees when the angels announced Christ's birth.
- Magnetic draw resembling what the wise men experienced in their search for the newborn King.

Quotables

What I'd like to have for Christmas
I can tell you in a minute.
The family all around me,
And the home with laughter in it.

EDGAR A. GUEST

Peace was the first thing the angels sang.
Peace is the mark of the sons of God.
Peace is the nurse of love.
Peace is the mother of unity.
Peace is the rest of blessed souls.
Peace is the dwelling place of eternity.

LEO THE GREAT

And all your kind and kinsmen,
That dwell both far and near;
I wish you a Merry Christmas,
And a happy New Year.

ANONYMOUS

But cold and selfish should we be,
And heartless, did we fail
To wish that you as well as we,
May merry be and hale!
May He whose love has ever blest
The righteous with its ray,
Grant you all good—and 'midst the rest
A merry Christmas Day!

WELSH TRADITIONAL CAROL

The Holy Night
The magi of the East, in sandals worn,
Knelt reverent, sweeping round,
With long pale beards, their gifts upon the ground,
The incense, myrrh, and gold
These baby hands were impotent to hold:
So let all earthlies and celestials wait
Upon thy royal state.
Sleep, sleep, my kingly One!

ELIZABETH BARRETT BROWNING

Christmas Prayer

O God, our loving Father, help us rightly to remember the birth of Jesus, that we may share in the song of the angels, the gladness of the shepherds, and the worship of the wise men. . .may the Christmas morning make us happy to be Thy children and the Christmas evening bring us to our beds with grateful thoughts, forgiving and forgiven, for Jesus' sake. Amen.

ROBERT LOUIS STEVENSON

Our Savior, the Dayspring from on high, has visited us,
And we who were in darkness and shadows have found the truth!

BYZANTINE PRAYER

Oh, thank You, Jesus, for being born for us, and living for us, and dying for us, and rising for us, and sending us the Holy Spirit. Thank You, with thanks beyond words, but most be expressed in the lovingness of our lives.

MADELEINE L'ENGLE

Jesus Christ was born:
Born in a stable,
Cradled in a manger,
In the world His hands had made,
Born a stranger.

CHRISTINA ROSSETTI

Christ is the one true Light that burns undimmed at the heart of Christmas. Santa Claus, Christmas trees, family gatherings, are all lesser planets that circle this one Star. They shine with bright beauty only when they reflect His light.

LUCIE CHRISTOPHER

What are we to make of Jesus Christ? . . . The real question is not what are we to make of Christ, but what is He to make of us?

C. S. LEWIS

Singables

For Christ is born of Mary;
And gathered all above,
While mortals sleep, the angels keep
Their watch of wondering love.
O morning stars, together
Proclaim the holy birth!
And praises sing to God the King,
And peace to men on earth.

PHILLIPS BROOKS

O come, O come, Emmanuel,
And ransom captive Israel,
That mourns in lonely exile here
Until the Son of God appear.
Rejoice! Rejoice! Emmanuel
Shall come to thee, O Israel.

LATIN HYMN

O star of wonder, star of night,
Star with loyal beauty bright,
Westward leading, still proceeding,
Guide us to thy perfect light.

JOHN H. HOPKINS

Flocks were sleeping, shepherds keeping,
Vigil till the morning new,
Saw the glory, heard the story,
Tidings of a gospel true.
Thus rejoicing, free from sorrow,
Praises voicing greet the morrow,
Christ the babe was born for you,
Christ the babe was born for you.

POLISH CAROL

Good Christian men, rejoice
With heart and soul and voice!
Give you heed to what we say:
Jesus Christ is born today.

GERMAN-LATIN CAROL

110

It came upon the midnight clear,
That glorious song of old,
From angels bending near the earth
To touch their harps of gold;
"Peace on the earth, good will to men,
From heaven's all gracious King."
The world in solemn stillness lay
To hear the angels sing.

EDMUND H. SEARS

As with gladness men of old
Did the guiding star behold;
As with joy they hailed its light,
Leading onward, beaming bright;
So, most gracious Lord, may we
Evermore be led to thee.

WILLIAM C. DIX

Joy to the world! the Lord is come:
Let earth receive her King;
Let every heart prepare him room,
And heaven and nature sing. . .

ISAAC WATTS

There's a song in the air!
There's a star in the sky!
There's a mother's deep prayer,
And a baby's low cry!

And the star rains its fire
while the beautiful sing,
For the manger of Bethlehem
Cradles a King!

JOSIAH G. HOLLAND

Scriptures

For to us a child is born, to us a son is given,
and the government will be on his shoulders.
And he will be called
Wonderful Counselor, Mighty God,
Everlasting Father, Prince of Peace.

ISAIAH 9:6

The people living in darkness have seen a great light;
on those living in the land of the shadow of death
a light has dawned.

MATTHEW 4:16

Glory to God in the highest, and on earth peace to men on whom his favor rests.

LUKE 2:14

The gift of God is eternal life in Christ Jesus our Lord.

ROMANS 6:23

But when the time had fully come, God sent his Son, born of a woman, born under law, to redeem those under law, that we might receive the full rights of sons.

GALATIANS 4:4–5

"Merry Christmas" in *Native Tongues*

Add a special touch to your greeting and say "Merry Christmas" in the form that the recipient is most used to seeing. They will appreciate your going to the trouble of finding out how to express your wish in their native language.

Dutch—*Vrolijk Kerstfeest*
French—*Joyeux Noël*
German—*Froehliche Weihnachten*
Greek—*Kala Christougenna*
Hawaiian—*Mele Kalikimaka*

Italian—*Buon Natale*
Pennsylvania German—
   En frehlicher Grischtdaag
Spanish—*Feliz Navidad*
Swedish—*God Jul*

Picture Message

Write your message with pictures that you draw or cut from magazines or old Christmas cards.

Word Picture

Print the message or letter in a shape on the page—Christmas tree, bell, circle, etc. Use a penciled-in template and old-fashioned typewriter, or give the challenge to those computer literate kids to keep them busy awhile!

Acrostic Message

Take a word like "Christmas" or "Noel" and place each letter on a descending line. Use each letter to start a line of sentiment. You can cut your letters out of fabric or contrasting paper, glue them to the card, and write beside them.

N - Nothing compares to the joy of Christmastime
O - Often I have thought of you, but
E - Each Christmas I want to let you know that you are
L - Loved and appreciated all year through.

It's a Wonderful Life

Even though we want our cards and letters to be positive and uplifting, not every thing in a year's time can be perfect. Blend the sad and imperfect happenings with the positive outlooks.

- Even though our car's engine blew in rush hour traffic, we met a neat man who drives a tow truck and started attending our church after Sis went on and on about our children's play.
- Even though our Thanksgiving trip to Grandma's was canceled because of the big snow storm and we had no turkey and trimmings in the house, we ordered pizza and made it a party in front of the fireplace.

Sympathetic

Holidays are especially hard for those who have lost a loved one. Send a card, but put a band-aid across the front of the picture. Inside, acknowledge how they must hurt, but that you remember and love them.

Daily Gift

In your card's message, include several scriptures for daily readings that will lead the recipient into the true meaning of Christmas.

I Love You

The most meaningful message that we often let go unsaid is "I love you." Don't let another minute go by without expressing your love to those who mean so much to you.

> *"They may forget what you said,*
> *but they will never forget how you made them feel."*

CARL W. BUECHNER

Reusing Christmas Cards

You are bound to get many cards in the mail from friends and family. It would be a shame to just throw them all away. Here are some clever ideas for reusing them.

Send a Second Time

Cut off the front flap of the card (as long as it doesn't have writing on the back). Use it as a postcard for a new greeting, a thank-you note, a party invitation, or a gift tag.

Frame

Find a card that has a beautiful border design. Cut a window in the card, keeping the border intact, and use it to frame a photo, poem, or something similar.

Ornaments

Cut the card's picture out in the shape of circles, stars, or other cookie cutter shapes. You could glue two of the same shape back to back for a sturdy, double-sided ornament. Add a bit of glue and a little glitter to make them shine. Put a hole and string in the top and hang them on your tree as ornaments.

Cover-ups

Wrap a box in plain paper and tape old card fronts all over it. If the box doesn't hint to the contents, then don't bother wrapping it before attaching the cards.

Bookmarks

Where the designs on card fronts cooperate, cut long narrow strips to use for bookmarks. You might want to laminate them for heavy use. Or write a message on the back and give to someone else to use. Insert a bookmark in a book when you give it as a gift.

Placemats

Get a piece of sturdy paper or poster board approximately 12"x16". Cut off several card fronts and/or cut out pictures from cards. Lay them in a design on the paper and lightly glue in place. Have it laminated or cover with clear contact paper. Use for a holiday placemat.

Coasters

Cut the card's picture out in the shape of circles, squares, octagons, hexagons, or the like. Use them under drinking glasses as disposable party coasters.

Place Cards

Find cards that have only pictures on the covers and sort out ones that have a large area that you can write on. Cut the card fronts off the old message part. Write the names of those in your dinner party on with marker or glitter pen. Lay the cards on each plate, insert them into the tines of the fork to hold them up, or prop them against the drinking glass.

Candle Wax Guards

If your church or organization is having a candlelit vigil for Christmas (or anytime really), cut old cards into circles. Cut an X in the middle where the small candlestick can be inserted.

Advent Calendar

Get a large piece of paper or poster board and number off sections 1–25. Start on December 1 and use a cutout from the old cards to mark off each day until Christmas. When the paper is full of pictures, Christmas has arrived.

Game

Create a concentration game for the kids to play on the long trip to Grandma's house. Gather 10–15 cards of the same size. Cut the picture in half. Mix the cards and lay them face down. Have the kids take turns trying to find matching cards. The one with the most matches wins.

Puzzle

Glue a card front to a piece of sturdy paper or cardboard. Then cut it into several puzzle pieces. Store individual puzzles in envelopes and use them to entertain the kids during holiday errands or on long road trips.

Sewing Cards

Punch holes in and around the picture/design of an old card front. Find a length of shoestring, yarn, or ribbon that will go around the perimeter of the card at least twice. Give to your preschoolers to play with.

Puzzle Card

Glue a card front to a piece of sturdy paper or cardboard. Write a message on the back of the picture, cut the pieces out, then mail them as a puzzle greeting card recipients will have to assemble to read.

Story Figures

Cut out large figures (Santa, animals, Nativity characters, etc.) from the cards. Glue sandpaper to the back of each and use them for stories on a felt board. Or glue a craft stick to the back of each one and let the kids use them as puppets. Or get a shoebox, paint a background inside, and put cardboard stands on the back of the pictures so they can be used as characters on the little stage.

Gift Boxes

Fold a large card to make a tiny gift box or tape several cards together to make a larger box.

Some of my best Christmas memories are of the simplest little things. . . ."

GWYNETH GAVIN

Creating Traditions

". . .do not forget the things your eyes have seen or
let them slip from your heart as long as you live.
Teach them to your children and to their children after them."

DEUTERONOMY 4:9

Answering Machine Greeting

Don't forget to put a Christmas touch to your away message on your phone and voice mail. Sing, quote Scripture, or give a Christmas blessing.

Plan an
"Eating and Greeting" Party

About three weeks prior to Christmas, get the whole family involved in preparing the Christmas greeting mailing. Divide the work into three areas: making the cards and/or personalizing the greeting, addressing the envelope, and sealing and stamping the envelopes. Part of the party can be a trip to the mailbox or post office. Of course,

you'll need to arrange to test some new Christmas goodie recipes at this event and end the evening with a good mug of hot chocolate.

Or do this with several friends or a church organization of ladies who all have Christmas greetings to prepare. Have lots of food to munch on. Prepare several workspaces. Tell guests to bring a basket or box to keep their cards, labels, stamps, and the like contained. Working with others to talk with makes the time enjoyable, and sharing tasks speeds up the process.

Banner Greeting

Create a banner with heavy paper, tarp, or an old bed sheet and some paint. Write a holiday greeting on it for your neighbors and others who drive by your house. Express your faith like "Love came down at Christmas" or "Jesus is the reason for the season." Hang it between two posts or along your porch railing.

Above and Beyond

Find a friend or neighbor who is overloaded with the pressures of the holiday and offer to help unload some of those pressures. Volunteer to address their Christmas cards. Run extra photocopies of a universal greeting card that they can use for their lists. Have them hand write their Christmas letter then type it and dress it up with artwork for them. Run to the post office for them.

Displaying Cards

Card Wall—Make a wall of cards. Cover all or part of a wall with plain-colored wrapping paper, a bed sheet, or inexpensive fabric. Then attach your cards as they come in using a pre-planned pattern.

Card Frame—Tape cards around doorframes, window frames, and picture and mirror frames.

Card Tree—Have a small tree designated as your card tree. As cards come in, use a paper punch to make a hole in the cards and tie on a ribbon hanger. Place the cards on the tree, and by Christmas Day your tree should be full of holiday cheer.

Card Wreath—Get a large foam wreath or cut one from a sheet of foam. Hang the foam on the wall, and as cards come in, pin them overlapping on the wreath.

Card Line—Run a length of string, ribbon, or twine around the room at head level or along the fireplace mantel. Hang cards on it with clothespins.

Card Fan—Use a paper punch to make a hole in the upper left-hand corner of each card. Then put them on a large key ring. Fan the collection out on the coffee table where family and guests can leaf through them.

Christmas Past Night

Take time out one night between Thanksgiving and Christmas to reflect on Christmases gone by. Dig out your collections of old Christmas cards that you just couldn't throw away, scrapbooks, photo albums, slides, home movies, treasured decorations, and the like. Invite older relatives to come and share their stories of Christmas in the Good Old Days.

Happy Birthday to Jesus!

Use this as your theme for the holiday season. Remind others of it as you personalize your cards. Use the birthday theme in your family newsletter. Embellish the letter with pictures of cakes, candles, balloons, streamers, and the like. Insert large metallic party confetti in your envelopes (confetti that will not be able to escape out of the seams). Have your children make cards to Jesus for His birthday to reinforce the true meaning of Christmas. Throw a birthday party on your tree trimming night. Have cake, ice cream, and all the birthday extras you can think about adding. Have guests bring a present for a child and donate the gifts to a child in need or an organization like Toys for Tots. Sing "Happy Birthday" to Jesus.

Card Shower

Work with your children or a Sunday school class to create beautiful homemade cards. Pick a nursing home to bless (and, if possible, get a list of names of the residents from the director). Take the children and deliver their Christmas mail from room to room. Include a treat that the nurses have approved with the card. The residents will certainly enjoy the attention you show them.

Caroling Card

Create a card with Luke 2 printed inside. Get your family's singing voices polished up and go door to door in your neighborhood. Sing favorite carols and leave a card with each household.

Love Jar

Write 7 or 14 reasons why you love your family (one per day leading up to Christmas) on small cards or strips of paper, and place them in a jar or candy dish. Each day at a meal, have a family member draw one and read a love greeting. Your family will have a continuous reminder of your love.

Letters to Your Children

Begin this year to write an annual letter to each one of your children at Christmastime—even if they are too young to read them right now. Review the highlights of the year for them and include praise for the accomplishments they have made (i.e. note their growth in inches or their batting average or their school grades). Express your love in words and let them know how proud you are to be their parent. Let the child read the letter, then be sure it gets stored away in a safe place. For young children, keep their collection of letters for them until they are fully grown.

Mail for the Kids

At a time when the mail picks up with Christmas cards and letters, the children might feel a bit left out. Send a Christmas card, letter, or gift through the mail to each of your children. Something stamped and delivered can seem more "official" to a kid than a hand-delivered sentiment. Or you could also mail your Christmas greetings to families under the names of their children. The kids would then get the rare chance to open mail. Tuck a piece of gum, balloon, or other item inside especially for them.

Remember Your Mail Carrier

Thank your mailman for handling the extra Christmas load and for good service all year long. Bake cookies or assemble a tin full of candies and leave it in the box for him or her.

Christmas Card Post Office

For a church fundraiser, set up a post office where church members send each other cards without having to mail them the traditional way. Have each person label their card clearly with the recipient's name and place them in a large box with a postage donation. You can charge a certain amount per card—ten cents per card could really add up—or ask for the full postage rate they would have spent using the US postal service. Have a team (youth group perhaps) sort the cards. Use lunch bags with each member or family name on it to hold the cards.

Photo Thanks

Take your time opening your Christmas gifts and enjoying the moment. Take pictures of the gifts that come from those who can't be there for the opening. Mount the picture on the front or inside of your thank-you notes. Bring the giver into the moment. For someone like Grandpa and Grandma, you might want to videotape the children opening their packages.

Family Thanks Night

As soon as possible after Christmas is over, plan a fun night when everyone in the family gathers their notepaper and writing supplies into one room of the house. Write your thank-you notes together and make it fun. Even the youngest member can get involved by drawing and coloring pictures of thanks. Let school-age children hand write their own thanks, misspellings and all. After someone finishes a thank-you that is ready to mail, they should get a "prize." Let them ring a little bell, have them do a stunt like a somersault or hand stand, or give them control of choosing the next song to play on the stereo.

Basketful of Prayer Reminders

Save cards received from others. At a meal once or twice a week through-out the year, take a card from the basket. Pray for that person/family. Send them a note, letting them know you've been thinking of them.

Christmas Scrapbook

After the holiday rush is over and the pictures are all developed, set aside an evening to put together a scrapbook. Perhaps you have a big book that you add to each year, or maybe you'd enjoy a small book for each year. Buy a book or hand-make it. Use an old Christmas card front for your scrapbook cover. Fold a stack of paper in half and staple the spine together. Then attach it to the card front. Use the pages to keep favorite Christmas greetings, photos, stories about special events, and so on.

*N*ow may the Lord of peace himself
give you peace at all times and in every way.
The Lord be with all of you."

2 THESSALONIANS 3:16